OAXACA

artisan • new york

"I remember going down to Mexico for the first time and immediately saying to myself, This is it."

—*Michael Schaible*
INTERIOR DESIGNER

Oaxacan Friezes

The imposing limestone walls at Mitla, dating to circa 900–1500, once protected the royal palaces and sacred burial sites 30 miles outside Oaxaca. Set within them are geometric and serpentine *grecas*, or friezes—said to represent Quetzalcoatl—which emulate pre-Columbian weaving patterns.

Metate

Used for centuries as a tool for grinding corn, the metate and its accompanying mano have found a niche in the design world. "They're still used in the villages," says designer Margarita Alvarez. "I often reference the shape in my projects—it helps me solve a great number of interior design issues."

continued on page 184

"I guess it is easy being green."

Presenting the **36** mpg Ford Escape Hybrid, the most fuel-efficient SUV on Earth.* How green is that?

www.fordvehicles.com

ESCAPE HYBRID

OAXACA

THE SPIRIT OF MEXICO

JUDITH COOPER HADEN

INTRODUCED BY PHIL BORGES

TEXT BY MATTHEW JAFFE

Published by Artisan
A Division of Workman Publishing, Inc.
708 Broadway
New York, New York 10003
www.artisanbooks.com

Library of Congress Cataloging-in-Publication Data

Haden, Judith Cooper.
Oaxaca : the spirit of Mexico / Judith Cooper Haden;
text by Matthew Jaffe.
p.cm.
ISBN 1-57965-214-X
1. Oaxaca (Mexico State)   I. Jaffe, Matthew.
II. Title.
F1321 .H33 2002
972'.740836'0222—dc21
2001056713

Printed in Italy
10 9 8 7 6 5 4 3 2 1
First Printing

Project consultant: Joseph Publishing Services, LLC

Book design by Dania Davey

PRECEDING PAGES: *Ancient frescoes and
fresh calla lilies adorn the entrance to the
renovated Santo Domingo convent that
now houses a luxury hotel in the heart of
downtown Oaxaca.*

RIGHT: *Interior courtyards yield sudden colorful
stuccoed surprises.*

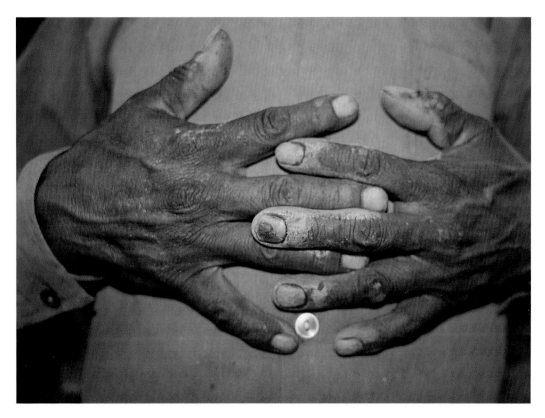

In memory of el Maestro Rodolfo Morales

Connection

A visit to Oaxaca in 1974 inadvertently opened for me an almost thirty-year exploration of the world's indigenous peoples—people who have lived and labored in the same place as countless generations have before them. Even though I've now visited dozens of cultures in remote places in the world, I'll never forget the initial feeling of being in a new place and a new culture. The commonplace took on a wonderful new twist. Birds flying overhead were parrots, colors were electric, smells were unfamiliar, and perhaps most unusual—the people were friendly. Although the novelty has diminished somewhat over the years, there is a feeling, which I can describe only as a sense of connection, that continues to resonate and draw me to new places where I can experience the feeling again.

Back then, as now, Oaxacans gathered every evening at the Zócalo. Watching them was like observing a human beehive—men in small groups making music together, women nursing babies and visiting while their children run and play, groups of old men gesticulating in animated debate while lovers walk arm in arm around the square, proudly parading their relationship before the community. It was a chaotic scene, but one that no one would consider missing.

By day, Oaxacans seemed even to enjoy the ride on broken-down buses crammed with people and animals shoved up on the roof. They talked and laughed, in spite of the dust and discomfort, and seemed more like a carefree group on a cruise than people going to and from their daily routines.

But it was only on my return home that I appreciated this quality of connection in Oaxacan life. Having taken a seat in a comfortable, air-conditioned bus for a two-hour ride to Sonoma in northern

California, I noticed that no one said a word and that all eyes were fixed on a newspaper or staring out a window. When we got to Sonoma, its historic town square was empty; everyone was at home. For the first time, all this seemed strange.

What is it about places like Oaxaca that foster this spirit of connection? Judith's photographs and Matthew's text are beautiful and sensitive windows into the fact that for Oaxacans—and other indigenous peoples—connection results from their fundamental relationship with the natural world. They believe that spirits—of the forest, mountains, animals, and their ancestors—sustain them, and that they have the responsibility to respect those spirits and be grateful to them or the consequences will be immediate and severe: Accidents will happen, children will get sick, crops will fail. Their daily rituals and traditions serve these beliefs.

Although to many of us this may sound like superstition, if we examine some of our own assumptions about nature, they appear to be based more on struggle and domination than on gratification and respect—man against the elements, man conquers the mountain, man has dominion over the animals. Which ideas would better enhance and promote connection?

After years of experiencing intact cultures all over the world, I recognize connection when I feel it. It is this feeling, I believe, that allows generation after generation to commit to their land, to their art, to one another. You can feel it in Oaxaca, and it is truly the spirit of Mexico.

Phil Borges

Phil Borges is a photographer, author, and the founder of Bridges, *an on-line classroom connecting indigenous children with their urban contemporaries.*

A hammock vendor hopes for a sale on Macedonia Alcalá Street.

CONTENTS

A pink-ribboned young girl sells flowers for altar decoration in the special Day of the Dead section of the Abastos market.

Imagination Revealed

Oaxaca is the Mexico of my vivid childhood imagination, first piqued at age nine or ten when my parents took me to Olivera Street in Los Angeles, and later fulfilled at twenty-one, when I stepped off a plane from the gray, staid Pacific Northwest and was immediately electrified by the colors, vibrancy, and graciousness that Mexico exuded.

Oaxaca attracts on so many levels: It is simultaneously colonial, pre-Columbian, and indigenous, and I'm never quite sure of just what I will find when I round a corner. It is impossible not to be drawn to the sedate, formal, ordered quality of the region's famous sixteenth- and seventeenth-century Spanish architecture. The old stone buildings, while not impervious to an earthquake's rumble, are somehow calming and reassuring. But these solid colonial masterpieces can sometimes obscure the fundamental fact that Oaxaca is still an ancient region that actively celebrates its remarkable native heritage.

It is a bustling, active part of daily life. Proud Zapotec and Mixtec families travel from the countryside to the city each day to sell their products, as they have for more than two thousand years. Attired in her traditional apron or an embroidered *huipil* (blouse), her long dark braids interwoven with yards of bright satin ribbon, a woman unloads her heavy goods from the basket she has carefully balanced on her head and takes her customary place in the market to start the long day of vying for sales. As a baby snuggles up in a soft black *rebozo* (shawl) while other children play nearby, she sits, serenely accepting her place in the universe. She is, in fact, doing exactly what her mother and grandmother have done before her.

A visit to a graveyard at any time of year, anywhere, offers quick clues to the values of a particular culture. Especially in Oaxaca, the importance of family anchors each new generation, reminding it of its place in a grander continuum. For the Day of the Dead, for example, large extended families reunite to tend to the needs of their ancestors. Yet even the least fortunate create elaborate home altars using ordinary household items and faded flowers to remind spirits to return home. This and other annual rituals of dance and death are restorative extravaganzas that bind families and whole villages together.

It is through the work of Oaxacan artists and artisans, however, that the drama of life and death and the presence of the ancient amid the modern truly find their most vivid and colorful expressions. For my photographer's eye, the folk art with its many seductive forms, enticing colors, and native materials becomes my own personal visual delight. The weathered faces and skilled hands of the creators speak of a determination to practice their crafts and to persevere in the face of occasional economic hardships and temptations of the technological world.

A traditional Mexican proverb proclaims: "What you don't see, the heart can't feel." And it is when I'm at home, editing images at the light table, that Oaxaca actually falls into perspective. Every transparency, whether depicting a tiny carved creature or a piece of ordinary pottery, a majestic cathedral or a child selling flowers, is a tangible expression of an ancient practice, of a tradition passed from generation to generation through an artist's hands, through thick stone walls, and through the commerce of the markets. A woman's beribboned braids persist, an enviable symbol of cultural constancy.

Tons of freshly cut yellow-gold marigolds herald the October 31 observance of Día de los Muertos (Day of the Dead).

With our rapidly changing ways and the instant technologies that govern our modern world, it is more critical than ever to celebrate this region and preserve its fragile traditions. The discouraging homogeneity and resultant economic inequities of the global economy have already begun to crack Oaxaca's tranquil demeanor. Despite the fact that tourism in Oaxaca has revitalized its ancient folk art traditions, it is only a matter of time before inexpensive mass-produced materials will cut into the artists' markets. Acrylic yarns are replacing cotton threads. Cheap imported plastic is replacing handmade pottery. Women's traditional *huipiles* are giving way to blue jeans and T-shirts; young people are more interested in putting their hands on a computer than in forming intricate clay pots.

With this book we celebrate the traditions and cultural heritage of a city and a region that is teetering on the edge of modernization. Local artists Francisco Toledo and Rodolfo Morales have decried the lack of a permanent museum of popular art in Oaxaca's central historic district, one that would preserve and honor the best of Oaxaca's folk heritage and remind each generation of the worth of these traditions. It is our hope that this book serves as a similar reminder to all peoples to preserve and nurture their cultural legacies.

Judith Cooper Haden

The city of Oaxaca and its surrounding towns and villages. Oaxaca State is shown in the inset map.

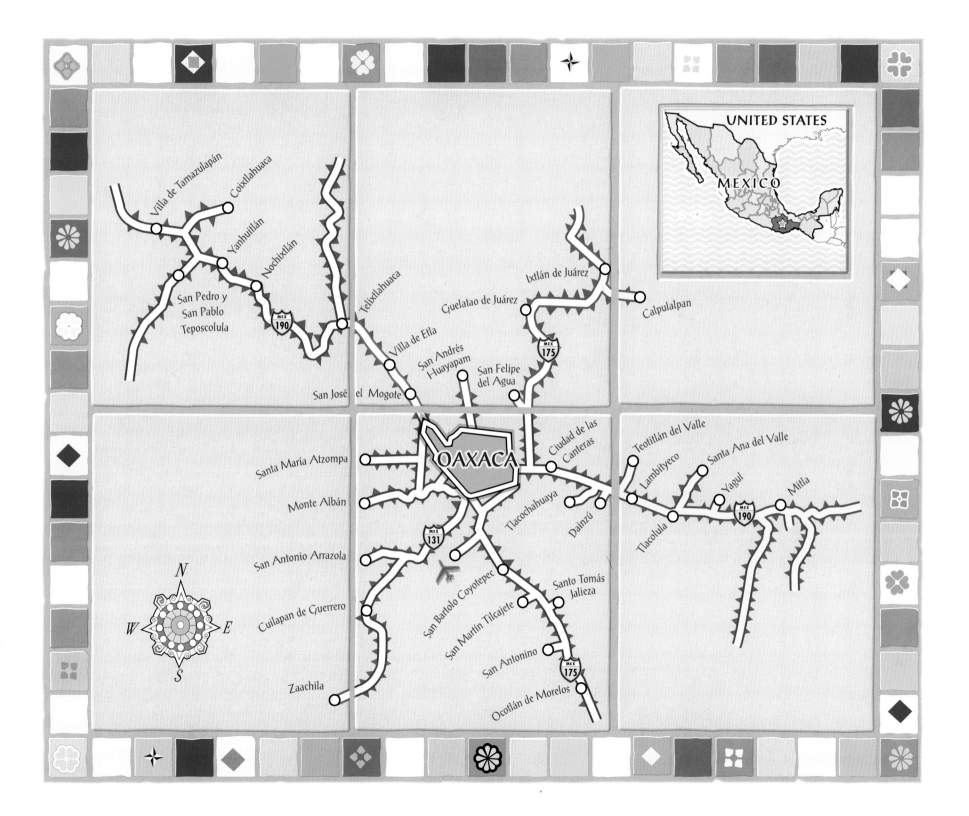

Por Más Que Dos Mil Años

For More Than Two Thousand Years

Monte Albán has seen nearly a million dawns. Day begins here as the morning's glow unfurls across the mountaintop, lighting the stone remains of Monte Albán's ceremonial buildings to a brilliant gold before the Valley of Oaxaca awakens from the darkness below.

Monte Albán rose approximately twenty-five hundred years ago, becoming the first city in North America. Before the Zapotecs, the original inhabitants of the area, flattened this mountaintop and began constructing a complex built of sandstone, limestone, and volcanic rock, the valley's people lived in scattered farming settlements. Monte Albán represented a colossal leap forward and became the political and religious center for a vast region.

At a time when London was little more than a collection of wood-and-thatch structures, and Venice was still hundreds of years from its founding, Monte Albán grew to be a city of seventeen thousand people. It endured as a capital for twelve hundred years, perhaps reaching a peak, between 300 and 700 A.D., of thirty thousand residents. As late as 1749, New York City had a population of just thirteen thousand.

These numbers tell only part of the story. There are places that feel like capitals, and Monte Albán is one of them. Walking about Monte Albán's plazas and along the steep, narrow stone steps of its temple platforms imparts the definite sense of having arrived at some central place.

Monte Albán is literally that, commanding the junction of the three branches that form the Y-shaped Valley of Oaxaca. The complex sits on almost a straight north-south axis. Though isolated by modern standards, Monte Albán was located at an important trading and cultural crossroads.

PRECEDING PAGE: *In the town of Zaachila in the Oaxaca Valley, this ancient bas-relief greets visitors who descend the steep staircase into the small excavated underground ruins.*

ABOVE: *The late-afternoon sun finally allows the warm stones to cool, asking one to linger among the immense ruins of the former city of Monte Albán.*

It was in no way immune to the ebb and flow of any other great civilization, however. Cultures rose and fell here: The Zapotec era gave way to Mixtec rule sometime after 900 A.D. The Aztecs marched south from their lands around today's Mexico City and conquered the Valley of Oaxaca in the fifteenth century, although Oaxacans continued to resist Aztec domination up until the Spanish conquest in 1521.

The conquest effectively ended thousands of years of a pure indigenous culture; the name Monte Albán itself is a Spanish creation. Monte Albán then languished on its mountaintop, worn down by wind and rain until the debris of the centuries finally buried the complex.

Today's city of Oaxaca grew from its roots as the Zapotec town of Huaxyacac and later an Aztec garrison to rise as Monte Albán's modern counterpart. Although it would eventually produce two of Mexico's most famous presidents, the Zapotec Benito Juárez and the Mixtec Porfirio Díaz, Oaxaca would never be the great political center that Monte Albán had been. But it remained a hub for regional trade and has evolved into a cultural capital for all of Mexico, preserving both the nation's Spanish and native legacies.

Its layout of tightly gridded streets around a central plaza is a classic of Spanish colonial architecture, and in 1987 the city was recognized by the United Nations as a World Heritage Site for its preservation efforts. Sixteen native languages and sixty dialects are still spoken in the state; Oaxaca remains deeply tied to its pre-Columbian past. Craftspeople in valley villages continue to produce pottery, weavings, and carvings, carrying its indigenous traditions into yet another millennium.

High above the valley, the grasses sprouting from the gaps between the stone steps at Monte Albán are a reminder that this ancient city, abandoned for a thousand years, is anything but a dead place.

A young boy in Tlacolula pauses at the immense 470-year-old doors to gaze inward at the Parroquia de la Virgen de la Asunción.

OPPOSITE: *Walking between the deserted buildings of Monte Albán, one longs for a clue to its sudden demise. Such a grand city it must have been!*

LEFT: *A probable descendant of the early Mixtec inhabitants, the young son of a modern-day groundskeeper looks for his father in the huge complex.*

ABOVE LEFT: *The family altar has a prominent place in the living room in most rural homes. Baby Jesus and other religious icons salvaged from San Antonino's church fire date back to the early 1900's.*

ABOVE RIGHT: *Treasured family photos and other personal mementos get a daily dusting from Josefina, their owner. Family photos are difficult to come by, and are highly regarded. Here, history is present, tangible.*

At a young ninety-three, Josefina Cornelio Córdoba was a treasured link to the past, a venerated craftswoman. Fearing the loss of her freedoms in marriage, she remained single and cared for her elderly mother and her family history. A highly regarded embroidery and crochet artist of traditional wedding garments, she made fine handwork until her recent death.

OPPOSITE AND FAR LEFT: *View from a courtyard of the surrounding countryside in full bloom at the former convent of San Juan Batista in Coixtlahuaca. Construction on this quiet, immense Dominican church, located to the northwest of the city of Oaxaca, began in 1546. The church is currently being restored.*

MIDDLE AND RIGHT:*The unfinished Dominican convent of Santiago in Cuilapan de Guerrero has glorious soaring arches and craggy mossy columns. It was the site of President Vicente Guerrero's execution in 1831.*

Clockwise from top left: *The luxurious interior courtyard of the former convent of Santa Catalina, now the Camino Real Oaxaca, soothes with blooming bougainvillea, manicured gardens, and the occasional twittering bird.*

Late-afternoon sun attracts vendors, students, and supplicants to Santo Domingo. The surrounding low stone walls provide a great perch for people-watching.

In the late 1500's, the majestic colonnade inside the San Juan Batista complex in Coixlahuaca saw monks and nuns scurrying down the corridor.

The working fountain within the restored Museo de las Culturas de Oaxaca (Museum of Oaxacan Cultures); the museum is justifiably Oaxaca's pride and joy.

A couple pauses to enjoy the city view from inside the Santo Domingo complex.

Building Oaxaca

With its fertile farmlands, mild climate, and position at a trading crossroads, the Valley of Oaxaca was a prominent region in New Spain from the earliest days of the Spanish conquest. So great was the area's appeal that in the 1520's Mexico's conquerer, Hernán Cortés, desired the valley for a kingdom of his own. He eventually received about three-hundred fifty thousand acres, although much to his dissatisfaction, the area where the city of Oaxaca now stands remained beyond his reach because the king had already granted that land to a group of colonists.

Oaxaca was laid out by the same architect who designed Mexico City and Veracruz. It stands among the best-preserved examples of Spanish colonial design in Mexico.

Many of the city's grandest structures were built by the Dominican order, which arrived in the late 1520's. The order constructed about 160 churches, as well as convents and housing, in the region. Aldous Huxley celebrated the church of Santo Domingo as "one of the most extravagantly gorgeous churches in the world." Some of the city's religious buildings have since been converted to other uses, including the convent of Santa Catalina, which now houses the Camino Real Oaxaca, and the convent at Santo Domingo, site of the cultural museum that holds the treasures from Monte Albán's Tomb 7, a Zapotec tomb appropriated in the fourteenth century for burial of a Mixtec king and his servants. Silver, turquoise, coral, jade, and, of course, gold were discovered there by Alfonso Caso in 1932.

While the look of Oaxaca is undeniably Spanish, indigenous influences are by no means absent. The city is built of local stone, notably used in the pale green- and rose-hued Basílica de Nuestra Señora de la Soledad. And, in her book *Zapotec*, Helen Augur notes that Oaxaca's architecture reflects the sensibilities of the Zapotec and Mixtec craftspeople who both influenced and executed the Spanish design, thus creating a distinctly Oaxacan style of colonial architecture.

Gold-leaf paint lavishly details the interior embellishments within the meticulously restored museum and cultural center at Santo Domingo. The nearby domed gilt ceilings seem to glow as one passes under them.

OPPOSITE LEFT: *The gentle colors and fine brush strokes of the original paint were carefully preserved on parts of the interior walls of the Museum of Oaxacan Cultures.*

OPPOSITE RIGHT AND ABOVE: *Stone from nearby quarries was used to construct much of the remarkable colonial architecture for which the city is famous. Many buildings have an identifying greenish cast due to the local origin of the stone. Here, a detail from the downtown Templo de San Felipe de Neri, decorated with garlands in honor of* Día de la Revolución (Day of the Revolution).

The Dominican monastery of San Jerónimo Tlacochahuaya was founded in 1586. Its interior painted ceiling is one of the true gems of colonial art in all of Mexico.

The Mitla archeological site, including its Group of Columns (far left), was built in 800 A.D. by the Zapotecs and appropriated next by the Mixtecs. The conquering Spanish Catholic archbishop of Oaxaca then added the adjoining red-topped church to the Mitla complex, seen peeking from a distance behind the ancient stone frieze (left). This small site reveals layers of history within its various architectural styles.

Personal history is revealed in the face of
Candelaria Durán Morales de Cruz from
San Juan del Estado. Of Mixtec origin,
Candelaria (pictured here at 101 or 102,
she wasn't quite sure), still weaves palm
frond baskets and walks them to town once
a week. Easily remembering Pancho Villa
and the Mexican revolution, which she felt
brought her family positive economic changes,
she also recalls the great famine and locust
plague of 1915 when they were forced to eat
cactus to survive.

Three views of stone frieze details at the archeological site of Mitla, c. 1350, in the Valley of Oaxaca. These motifs appear again and again in the region's folk art, and even in Candelaria's baskets, which appear in the background, opposite.

ABOVE: *Graceful calla lilies are everywhere in Oaxaca. These bundles, intended for grave decoration and beautification, were photographed outside Oaxaca's Panteón General, a public cemetery, on the outskirts of town.*

OPPOSITE: *Heavy wooden doors and ornate hardware typify colonial architecture and lead into the tiled colonial church at Mitla. The handmade beeswax ceremonial candles are made in Teotitlán del Valle, and each leaf is individually molded and attached by artisans working in centuries' old techniques.*

A welcoming antique carved wooden greeter
has graced the entryway to the church at Mitla
for centuries.

FAR LEFT: *Door hardware detail, at the Parroquía de la Virgen de la Asunción in Tlacolula.*

LEFT: *Restored walls and windows within the sixteenth-century Templo de Santo Domingo in Ocotlán de Morelos. Local soil used in the final burnished topcoat of stucco gives the walls a glowing vanilla-cream color.*

RIGHT: *Seventeenth- and eighteenth-century carved wooden saints from home altars often find their way into antiquities shops in the historical section of the city of Oaxaca.*

OPPOSITE: *The unrestored part of the small, decorated colonial church at Macuilxochitl, next to Teotitlán del Valle.*

*Stone angels add a bit of levity to the solemn
San Juan Batista convent in Coixtlahuaca.*

Rodolfo Morales

There was a sweetness to Oaxacan artist Rodolfo Morales, a patience and self-effacement that was perhaps unexpected in an artist regarded as one of the most important figures in contemporary Mexican art.

Growing up, he was the outcast, but from that isolation grew a clear vision that his fellow Oaxacan artist Rufino Tamayo recognized early. "His voice, although it is a quiet voice, now begins to be heard, because it has something to say and says it in a convincing way."

Morales's demeanor rarely revealed the determination and commitment that he brought both to his art and the restoration work that Fundación Cultural Rodolfo Morales performed on more than a dozen buildings in the village of his birth, Ocotlán. He maintained a studio in Ocotlán in a restored colonial house. With the morning light pouring in through large second-floor windows, Morales would begin his long days by working on collages before turning to the oil paintings that reconfigure the Mexico he knew into something both recognizable and magically new. Despite the surreal nature of his work, Morales said it came not from his dreams as much as from hard work. "I don't believe much in inspiration," he said. "I believe in discipline."

Morales made that remark a little more than a month before his death in January 2001. His voice was particularly soft that day, but his passion remained strong. He expressed little concern about how others would remember him. But he did hope that his foundation's work would be carried on by the young people who learned restoration techniques through his efforts.

Although a believer in computer technology, Morales lamented the impact that modernization was having on the local culture. He found reason for hope in the women of Oaxaca, one of his favorite artistic subjects. "The most authentic thing about Oaxaca is its primitive quality," he said. "Even though the city has evolved a lot, it still has the women: With their faces, their braids and colored ribbons and embroidered blouses—the ones that you see in the market. They know only how to be Oaxaqueñas."

OPPOSITE: *A town meeting in the mayor's office in Ocotlán is enveloped by murals painted by Rodolfo Morales. A Mexican tradition since the revolution, public murals by famous painters belong to and are available for the permanent enjoyment of all the people within the community.*

ABOVE: *Lost in his work in his studio at the Casa de Cultura in Ocotlán, Morales painted by morning light, surrounded by his tubes of paint and the songs of birds outside his second-story window. His assistants would chat with him as he painted, while he made decisions regarding his exhibitions and the sale of his work.*

The gold-leaf-painted exterior detail of the restored Templo de Santo Domingo in Ocotlán de Morelos is typical of the nine regional churches restored by the Fundación Cultural Rodolfo Morales. The cost of the renovation was underwritten primarily by the maestro himself, from the international sales of his paintings. Gold and silver from the mines at Santa Catarina Minas financed the original construction.

Proud of Morales and the remarkable work of his foundation, local pottery artists create a ceramic replica of the Templo de Santo Domingo in Ocotlán (right) for use in a Christmas Nativity scene.

ABOVE: *A wall of family niches at the Panteón General (General Cemetery) invites a stroll down the interior corridor to examine the hand-inscribed names and dates of those buried here.*

RIGHT: *Wrought iron gates cast long shadows onto the plaque commemorating the four-year-long restoration of the Museum of Oaxacan Cultures in downtown Oaxaca.*

EL 17 DE ENERO DE 1994 LA SECRETARIA DE LA DEFENSA
NACIONAL ENTREGO LAS INSTALACIONES DEL
EXCONVENTO DE SANTO DOMINGO DE GUZMAN,
QUE OCUPO EL EJERCITO MEXICANO POR MAS DE
UN SIGLO Y FUERON RESTAURADAS ENTRE 1994 Y 1998
CON EL CONCURSO DEL GOBIERNO FEDERAL A TRAVES
DEL CONSEJO NACIONAL PARA LA CULTURA Y LAS ARTES
Y EL INSTITUTO NACIONAL DE ANTROPOLOGIA
E HISTORIA; DEL GOBIERNO CONSTITUCIONAL
DEL ESTADO DE OAXACA, DE FOMENTO SOCIAL
BANAMEX A.C; Y DE PRO-OAX A.C.

EL CENTRO CULTURAL SANTO DOMINGO FUE
INAUGURADO EL 24 DE JULIO DE 1998 POR EL
C. PRESIDENTE DE LOS ESTADOS UNIDOS MEXICANOS.

LA SOCIEDAD OAXAQUEÑA DA TESTIMONIO DE SU
RECONOCIMIENTO A LOS CONSTRUCTORES
ORIGINALES DE ESTE MONUMENTO HISTORICO
Y A LOS OBREROS, ARTESANOS Y ARTISTAS QUE
TRABAJARON EN SU RESTAURACION.

Corazón del Pueblo

Heart of the City

Oaxaca is busy, but not so busy that its details don't emerge. The songs of canaries and parrots drift from hidden courtyards out over the city. They are joined by a rapid whisking sound as a shopkeeper grips the rough wood handle of a twig broom, and sweeps the dust from the sidewalk out toward the cobblestone street. Bound for the Zócalo, visitors and residents stroll past him, down straight streets lined by low-slung, thick-walled colonial buildings, many hundreds of years old.

The sun casts sharp shadows against the freshly painted cobalt walls of one structure, lighting the weathered and peeling green door of another, and revealing patches of orange paint underneath. Wall-sized, hand-painted advertisements splash more bold color across the city and seem more committed to art than sales.

There is both an order and a magic to moving around the city; people seem to settle into a personal orbit propelled by a combination of practicality, curiosity, and impulse. Paths periodically cross and then recross, creating moments of surprise tempered by the sense that nothing that happens in Oaxaca is entirely random.

A tiny old woman seen one afternoon squeezing onto one of the crowded buses that runs between the city and the outlying villages is spotted two days later bargaining for fruit at the Abastos market. An American tourist, gone native in *huipil* and deep into her Frida Kahlo fantasy, strolls the Zócalo on Tuesday and then is seen cooing over the stuffed squash blossoms at a restaurant on Thursday night. It happens time and time again: A face disappears from a balcony decorated with ornamental ironwork only to reappear a few days later, eyes uplifted in prayer before the altar at the seventeenth-century Basílica de Nuestra Señora de la Soledad.

For all its history, Oaxaca doesn't feel like a museum, with its objects embalmed for the sake of preservation. Its churches can certainly be appreciated purely as objects of religious art: statues of Dominican martyrs holding their own heads, the soaring gold-leaf interior of the baroque sixteenth-century church of Santo Domingo. But they gain their real power from the role that they continue to play for the region's residents. There is the hope and faith of that praying woman. And there are the memories of an old man who points out the church where as a boy seventy years earlier he rang bells and polished candlesticks. Each morning he would walk his great-grandmother to the church. She lived to ninety-nine, and he's well on his way.

As night falls, people gather at the Zócalo and in restaurants and cafés around town. In one spot not far from Santo Domingo, a group plays the *sones* of nearby Veracruz State. The sweet melodies pour into the street, luring passersby who come in, then sit transfixed by the music as the shadows of candle flames dance off the tawny, plastered walls.

The *sones* linger in the mind, flowing straight into dreams. Then long after midnight, those gentle songs are replaced by a far brasher sound as a brass band, its night still not quite over, marches down a street and past a hotel. Two foreigners appear on their hotel balconies, watching in silence until the procession turns a corner. Then they begin to talk in the cold air under the stars, both struggling to remember just where they had seen the other before.

All day long the Zócalo is alive with people, from the businessman having his shoes shined to tourists in cafés, to happy celebrants or political protesters parading and demonstrating. The city's largest parade occurs on November 20 and commemorates the Mexican revolution of 1910.

Zócalo

Beneath the shade of Indian laurel trees and to the sounds of a marimba band, life in Oaxaca plays out on a glorious yet intimate civic stage. Centered on an elevated, round-roofed bandstand and with arcaded walkways, the cathedral and government buildings forming its borders, the Zócalo lures both tourists and locals eager to settle into the rhythms of the day. For the price of a hot chocolate at a café, or for free on a park bench, you can watch the coy ballet of young lovers on a Sunday afternoon, or the heated, hand-waving discussions of old men who never agree on anything—except to come back to the Zócalo and start all over again the next day. A cluster of shimmering balloons floats lazily near the cathedral, while a group of protesters settles in for the night across from the Palacio de Gobierno (Governor's Palace). The Zócalo has a long tradition of political demonstrations, some of which have helped topple state governors.

When asked about this protest, a man shrugs. "They want better water, better schools. Lots of things." A little girl, maybe eight years old, approaches tourists at one of the cafés. She is wearing traditional native dress, but her plaid school uniform peeks out from beneath it. When someone buys one of her straw weavings, she lingers at the table for a long time. Her dark eyes reflect the streetlights as she describes her village and talks about her dreams.

Above left: *A friendly local landmark, the "Catrina" sculpture by Mexico City artist Miguel Linares welcomes passersby from above at a popular folk art shop.*

Above right: *A weathered street poster depicting Pancho Villa invites locals to a political gathering. Political demonstrations and weeks-long vigils outside the Palacio de Gobierno are an ongoing part of the landscape of the city.*

Opposite: *Worn posters on ancient walls forge a new genre of popular "found" art.*

er Aniversario de la Masacre de

28 d

Color punctuates the inner city, appearing at every bend of the road with sudden intensity—on residential stuccoed walls, in storefront businesses, and in bursts of bougainvillea and jacaranda blooms.

Even ubiquitous corporate logos seem a bit more palatable, as in this huge hand-painted advertisement.

RIGHT: *A reinterpretation of classic eighteenth- and nineteenth-century serape designs by master carpet weaver Arnulfo Mendoza. This example, found in a downtown gallery, displays the intricate weaving of wool, silk, and gold thread.*

OPPOSITE: *A serious and hard-working young Oaxacan boy plays the accordion for tips in the historic district.*

Francisco Toledo

In the middle of an interview at his Graphic Arts Institute near Santo Domingo, Francisco Toledo receives a call from his fellow Oaxacan artist Rodolfo Morales. Morales is feeling ill and is seeking assistance finding a doctor. Toledo offers advice and with it comes a discourse on the environment that then segues into a lengthy discussion on a variety of Oaxacan evils, from burning tires to the construction of two-story buildings in the 1950's.

While best known as Mexico's greatest living artist, Toledo is also deeply involved in protecting Oaxaca's cultural legacy and building one for the future. Over the years, he has fought against hotels and parking lots that threatened to devastate the city's historic heart. He has helped fund libraries, a photography center, and the environmental and cultural preservation group Pro-OAX. His efforts are made possible through the sales of his internationally celebrated art, a blend of Mexican folkloric images and the stylistic influences of such twentieth-century European artists as Paul Klee and Joan Miró, and Oaxacan master Rufino Tamayo.

Despite both his philanthropic and creative successes, Toledo remains the rebel and iconoclast. His clothes are worn and typically splattered with paint. He walks about Oaxaca in a pair of sandals, and his eyes have a teasing gleam. He likes to chide those Oaxaqueños who he feels embraced indigenous art only after it became fashionable.

With popularity come risks to the art's integrity, says Toledo. "The demand is so great that at times the quality is suffering. Too many shops, too much demand. The artists are in too much of a hurry."

OPPOSITE: *The new Photographic Center Alvarez Bravo is due to the generosity of Maestro Toledo. There are classrooms, visiting photography professionals, and galleries, as well as a bookstore/gift shop.*

BELOW LEFT: *Maestro Francisco Toledo at sunset, high above the city he so passionately supports.*

BELOW RIGHT: *Inside the Graphics Arts Institute, which hosts a research library, museum/gallery, and café—another gift of Toledo.*

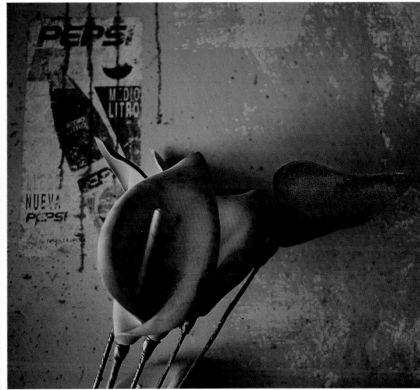

As the heat of the day subsides, the late-afternoon light draws Oaxacans back outside and electrifies Oaxaca's many extraordinarily colorful facades.

PRECEDING PAGES: *An afternoon squall during the rainy season (May to October) transforms a colonial building's seemingly immutable façade. Every city block is busy with carpenters repairing and renovating, painting and hammering, to keep the historic district fresh.*

LEFT: *The local* comida corrida *is the big meal of the day: It is a fixed-price lunch, replete with soup, meat, vegetables, dessert, and drink.*

As the day winds down on the Zócalo, balloon sellers begin to appear in large numbers, attracting parents with children. Several times a week, the bandstand is home to free midday and evening concerts given by the state brass band and marimba orchestras. Active for more than 150 years, the state band was begun by French and Austrian musicians sent to Mexico at the time of Emperor Maximilian (1864–1867).

Mixing metaphors: Religious figurines, imported amusements, and the locally brewed mezcal all share a shelf quite comfortably.

Evenings bring music, laughter, and much revelry on the Zócalo. Minstrels, either individually or in groups, wander from table to table in hopes of tempting the café's patrons to bargain for a tune or two. Another night, a brother-and-sister act builds a human pyramid, expecting onlookers' applause and perhaps a tip.

ABOVE: *Christmas lights on the Governor's Palace on the Zócalo illuminate the night, inviting strollers to visit booths of local artisans selling their crafts.*

RIGHT: *During the day of December 23, thousands of curious onlookers flock to view the carefully constructed displays of carved radish sculptures and cornhusk doll imagery at the annual* Noche de los Rábanos *(Night of the Radishes). By night, holiday shoppers sample fresh* tortas *made of Oaxacan string cheese,* bolillos *(bread rolls), deep-fried pastries called* buñuelos, *as well as Oaxaca's famous fruit candies for dessert.*

Hecho
a Mano

PRECEDING PAGE: *Josefina Cornelio Córdoba proudly displays the very last of her embroidery creations, an intricately stitched Oaxacan wedding dress. Her expertise and fame spread far outside Mexico, and she was busy filling special orders for her original creations until her death at age ninety-four. She painstakingly combed and braided her long hair to be ready to be photographed at her home in San Antonino.*

ABOVE: *Posed in front of the family altar with his parents and grandparents, Bulmaro Pérez Mendoza and his wife, Aura Bautista Lazo, are third-generation carpet weavers from Teotitlán del Valle. Bulmaro speaks three languages, as do many of the young weavers: Spanish, English, and the local Zapotec dialect.*

Made by Hand

"The Mexican people express themselves with their hands," artist Rodolfo Morales said. "The artisan gives much of himself, even in the simple weaving of a frond basket."

Morales's assessment was confirmed a few years back during a visit with basket maker Candelaria Durán Morales de Cruz of San Juan del Estado. Even at one hundred years old, Candelaria remained involved in each stage of the basket-making process. She spoke of going into Oaxaca to buy palm fronds, which she then carried back to her village on a two-hour bus trip—a vast improvement over the night-long, twenty-mile trips she once made by oxcart. She collected her own firewood, then smoked the palm fronds herself to create darker material for an alternating decorative pattern. Her hands still strong and graceful, Candelaria said it took her two days to weave each basket. Once they were completed, she would walk to the next town to sell them.

Candelaria is part of a tradition that has made the Valley of Oaxaca one of the great centers for crafts and folk art anywhere in the world. Its history reaches back more than two thousand years to the golden age of Monte Albán, but its materials and styles incorporate those that arrived with the Spaniards.

Reminiscent of Bali, many villages specialize in a single craft, from the rich red cochineal–dyed woolen weavings of Teotitlán del Valle and the woven cotton belts and sashes made on backstrap looms in the homes of Santo Tomás Jalieza to the emerald-green glazed pottery produced in Atzompa. Styles and media certainly vary but virtually every piece reflects a common set of traits: an artist's mastery, a link to the past, and an equally strong bond with the land. In the village of San Bartolo Coyotepec that happens to be literally true.

Renowned for a distinctive unglazed black pottery, the village depends on the local clays for its livelihood. Not surprisingly, the villagers are very protective of their most important natural resource: The town owns the mine where the clay is found, and will not sell it outside Coyotepec. And some locals still hold to a superstition that if a woman goes into the mine, there will be more stones in the clay, which even under the best circumstances takes weeks to bring to the proper consistency.

There is something almost magical about watching a veteran potter at work. Instead of a wheel, she uses a pair of saucers. Stooping on the bare ground, she inverts the bottom one to create a base, and places a previously formed rough clay cylinder on the upper saucer. She spins the upper saucer with one hand and uses a wet piece of leather to shape the clay from the inside. Her fingers move as deftly and rythmically as any musician's.

She then rounds the form a bit more with a piece of bamboo before incising the clay with a decorative semicircular pattern. She lets the piece dry for days before she burnishes and fires it in a covered, underground kiln, where the gray-green clay is transformed to a black finish. There are no gauges: Only the color of the kiln's flame is her guide.

CLOCKWISE FROM TOP LEFT: *Tinsmith Miguel Aguero Pacheco hammers a small floral design. Alebrije painters decorate their wooden creations at ARIPO, the state-run folk art shop in Oaxaca city. In Arrazola, famed carver Miguel Jiménez still carves occasionally. Potter Delores Porras is credited with the popular applied design movement on the decorative pottery of nearby Atzompa. Carpet weaver Felipe González, from Teotitlán, holds the tools of his trade. In Teotitlán del Valle, Sofia Ruiz creates beeswax flowers for ceremonial candles.*

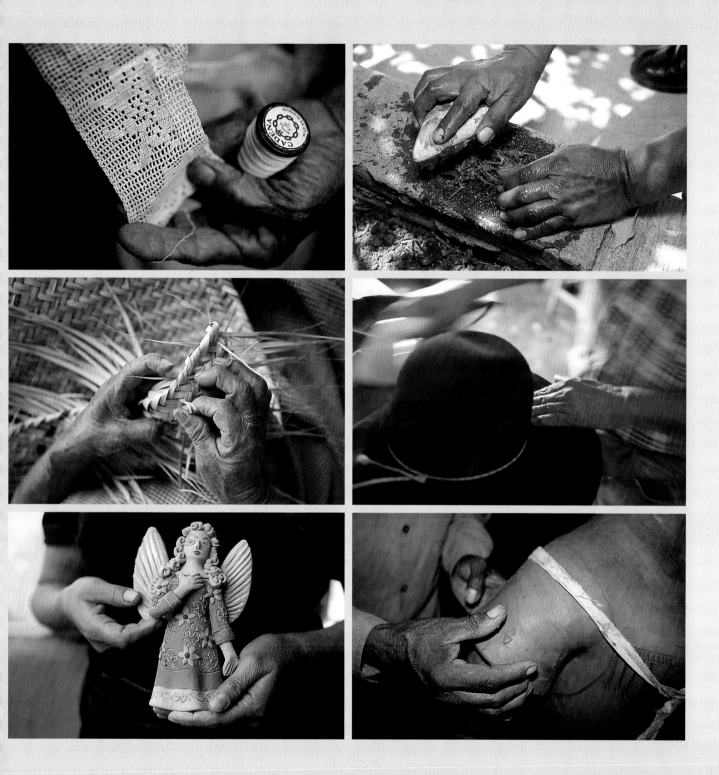

CLOCKWISE FROM TOP LEFT: *Josefina Cornelio Córdoba demonstrates her intricate crochet work. Isaac Vásquez's assistants extract indigo dye to color wool for carpets. Hatmaker Juan Vargas Luna uses antique French wooden forms to create felt hats. Juan Antonio García molds the arms of a new clay creation. Angelíca Vásquez, potter extraordinaire from Santa María Atzompa, holds one of her signature angels. Fingers still nimble at one hundred, Candelaria Durán Morales de Cruz weaves palm fronds into baskets.*

Chipper at age seventy-eight, Fidel Sánchez Martínez happily sold his handmade paper fans and banners under the giant fig tree on Sunday mornings outside the famous church in Tlacochayuaya.

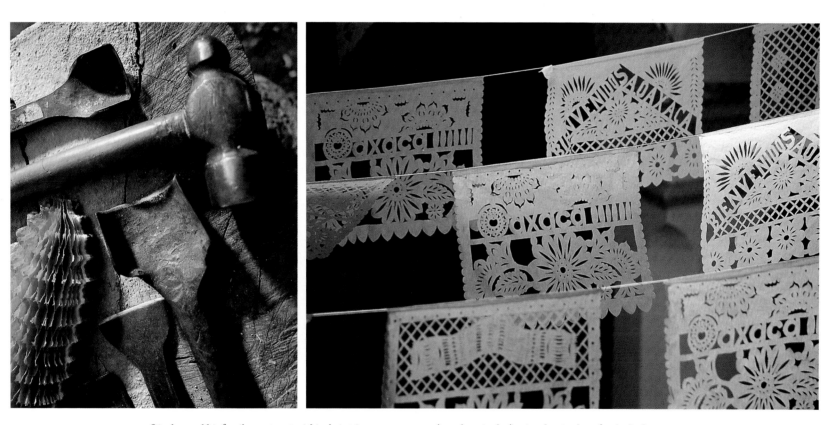

Sánchez and his family create astonishingly intricate paper cutouts (papeles picados) using the simplest of tools. In Oaxaca, these elaborate banners welcome visitors at the state tourism office near the main cathedral.

RIGHT: *In Arturo Sosa's home workshop, complex tinwork is hand-pounded by family members and neighbors. Colorful hand-painted tin hearts are a specialty.*

FAR RIGHT: *Miguel Aguero Pacheco's workshop has orders stacked up ready for export. The successful women's cooperative MARO (in English, Women Artisans from the Regions of Oaxaca) sells quality crafts from the entire state. Goods are left on consignment, and commissions are paid daily if need be.*

OPPOSITE: *The simple tools of the trade for Oaxacan tinsmith Pacheco and his family.*

LEFT: *For the family carpet business, Margarita Méndez Bautista cards the sheep's wool before spinning and dying it with natural dyes. The family has been creating traditional hand-loomed carpets in Teotitlán del Valle for three generations. Descendants of the original sheep brought by the colonizing Spaniards are still producing wool for the village, although longer, more stable fibers are being imported from other countries as competition for export sales increases.*

OPPOSITE: *The lowly cochineal bug (Dactylopius coccus) feeds off its host, the nopal cactus, in the Tlapanochestli bug farm near Santa María Coyotepec.*

Cochineal bug

It is only appropriate that Oaxaca's most prosperous era was born of a desire for beauty.

From 1750 to 1810, Oaxaca was the world capital for cochineal export. Cochineal is a strong dye produced from a scale insect that lives on nopal cactus. The red dye is produced after the female insects are ground and dried; it takes seventy thousand insects to make one pound of dye.

While indigenous people were using cochineal for centuries, it was unknown in Europe. Cochineal was first shipped to Spain in 1526, shortly after the conquest, and soon became the dye of choice, being many times stronger than any other known source. As the European textile industry grew in the eighteenth century, Oaxaca's cochineal trade became increasingly profitable. The brilliant wool robes of European royalty were dyed with cochineal, as were the red coats of the British army. Cochineal was New Spain's most coveted export after gold and silver.

The cochineal trade declined with the introduction of synthetic dyes in the nineteenth century. While artificial dyes remain cheaper and therefore popular, traditional craftspeople still value cochineal for its richness and permanence. In fact, there has been a resurgence in the use of cochineal in Teotitlán, and now a research farm operates in the valley, in addition to scattered local nopal patches. Other natural sources, including lichens for yellows and browns and indigo for purples, are used along with cochineal as dyes.

Yarn for individually loomed carpets is dyed naturally using tints extracted from lichens, cochineal bugs, walnut shells, alfalfa, pomegranates, marigolds, indigo, and mollusks. The color is set with a lime-and-water mixture, air-dried, and then washed with soap. This yarn, ready for weaving, was found at the Galería Mano Mágica in Oaxaca city.

Above left: *Master weaver Isaac Vásquez is credited with helping to popularize the pictorial carpet weaving genre by introducing complicated designs, which can often take several months to complete.*

Above right and opposite: *Modern-day large wooden looms use the same structural elements as those introduced by the Spaniards centuries ago. Traditionally, the upright treadle loom is men's work, while women are relegated to the smaller, more lightweight and portable backstrap loom. Here, Felipe González demonstrates his craft in Teotitlán del Valle. González, his sons, and extended family members produce lovely muted carpets for sale locally as well as for international export. As many as twenty to thirty family members can be employed by one lead weaver in what is now a booming community business.*

Carpets of every size, shape, and color can be found in the city of Oaxaca, Teotitlán del Valle, Santa Ana del Valle, as well as at the weekly regional markets.

Potter Juan Antonio García, his wife, and family pose with one of their large, colorful creations in San Antonino, just outside Ocotlán de Morales.

At work in his dimly lit studio, Juan Antonio García creates glorious life-size statues using his wife as his model. His figurative pieces are easily distinguishable by the mole he places between a figure's eyes.

OPPOSITE: *One of Juan Antonio García's natural clay mermaids.*

FAR LEFT: *Potter Josefina Aguilar, in her studio at the entrance to Ocotlán, is one of Isaura Aguilar's four daughters, whose ceramics have achieved international popularity with collectors. Each sister has a distinctive, easily recognizable style.*

LEFT: *In the town of Santa María de Atzompa, another pottery style was popularized by, among others, Delores Porras, shown here at age seventy-five. Suffering from diabetes, she tires more easily now, but she has taught her children how to create her whimsical mermaid and fish platters, as well as her more elaborate female figures.*

RIGHT: *The embellished green pottery from Santa María de Atzompa is used here at the immense La Capilla restaurant near Zaachila in the valley.*

FAR RIGHT: *Concepción Aguilar's hand-painted sign invites visitors to her new studio, located across the road from those of her sisters.*

OPPOSITE: *Mounds of seemingly indestructible and inexpensive pottery for everyday use is displayed in the handicrafts section of the Abastos market near the Oaxaca bus station.*

Black pottery (barro negro) is the specialty of Valente Nieto, son of legendary Doña Rosa in San Bartolo Coyotepec. Doña Rosa pioneered the craft of making big pots without using a pottery wheel, just two saucers. The distinctive silvery black color of the pots appears during the reduction firing of the clay.

Oaxaca's patron saint, the Virgin of Solitude, resides in the downtown church, her solid-gold crown weighing a reputed five pounds! Above are various representations of the beloved Virgin: Interiors of the baroque Basílica de Nuestra Señora de la Soledad; artists' renditions of Soledad in two clay replicas; carved in radishes at the Noche de los Rábanos exhibition; in painted plaster of Paris in a religious gift store; and a dried flower creation by famed Timoteo Godínez.

La Soledad

Pausing outside the carved façade of Basílica de Nuestra Señora de la Soledad, an old Oaxaqueño lowers his voice, his tone a mixture of reverence and wonder as he explains the legend of Oaxaca State's patron saint.

The miracle happened in 1543. A mule train—some say from Guatemala, others from Veracruz—was en route to Oaxaca when it stopped near town for the night. When dawn came, the driver noticed that a thirteenth mule bearing a large box had joined the dozen mules of his pack train. Accounts vary, as they will with legends, he adds, but most agree that the mule stopped and refused to move past the Hermitage of San Sebastián. The mule drivers removed the heavy box and the animal took a few steps, then dropped dead.

The Oaxaqueño points to a stone just inside the basilica's entrance, where the mule is said to have died. There, he continues, upon opening the box, the men discovered a statue of Christ and the carved head and praying hands that a note identified as the Virgin of Solitude.

It was decided that a church should be built on the spot where the miracle took place. Constructed in the seventeenth century, the basilica that stands here today is not the original church but a fitting home for Soledad. She presides from the main altar, dressed in a gown adorned with the pearls given as tribute by the sailors her miracles are said to have saved.

The Oaxaqueño looks up at the Virgin, then at the angels who seem to float above the nave. "I used to look at those angels all the time," he says. "I thought they were real. Just in the air. Flying angels."

The Benito Juárez market in downtown Oaxaca offers stall upon stall of handmade crafts, including huipiles, hammocks, and treadle-loomed textiles. There are amazing variations of the traditional shawl called the rebozo, woven in cotton, acrylic, or rayon in varying degrees of quality as well. Here, a vendor keeps busy by embroidering.

Far left: *Trique weaver María Flores de Jesús and her daughter Verónica sell their weavings in the former Carmen el Alto outdoor market. Known for their distinctive red-striped wool huipiles, Triques number about fifteen thousand people and dwell in a small area northwest of Oaxaca city.*

Left: *A demonstration of backstrap loom weaving by a seventy-four-year-old Trique weaver. These newer designs are created with the tourist in mind and are a recent departure from traditional patterns.*

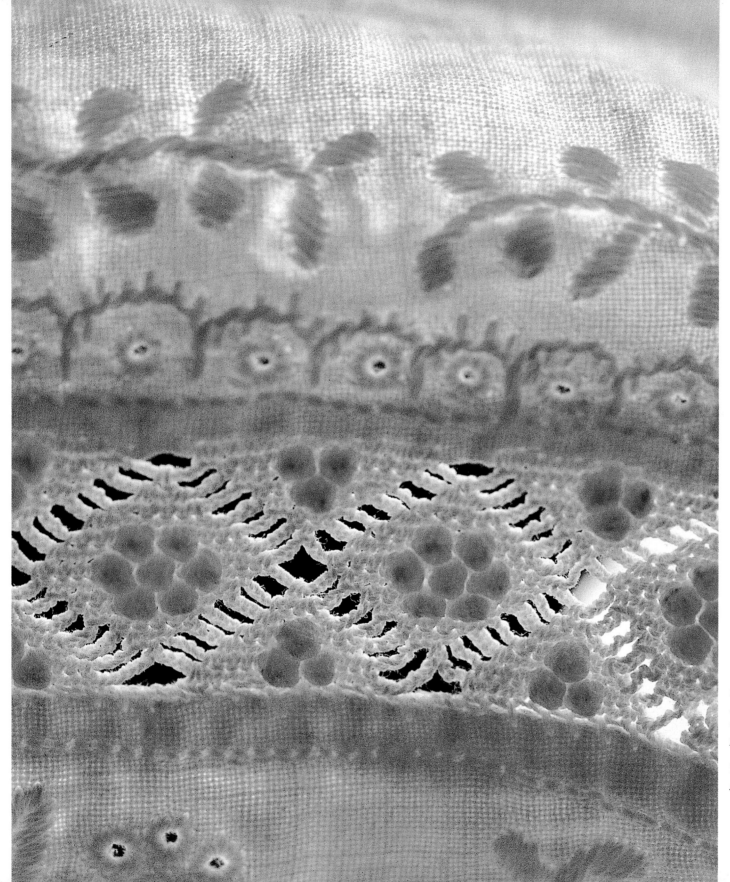

OPPOSITE: *Basket detail by Candelaria Duran Morales de Cruz, whose designs use both natural and smoked, darkened palm fronds.*

LEFT: *Detail of a blouse handmade by Josefina Cornelio Córdoba.*

RIGHT: *In Arrazola, an entire town has prospered greatly due to the popularity of its tiny carved wooden figures,* alebrijes, *which are made primarily of copal wood gathered near the town. Family home-studios welcome both locals and tourists alike to watch artisans, such as seventeen-year-old Fidel Mendoza Ibañez, work hard at their craft, or to buy animals for their collections. The carvers allow the shape of the wood to dictate the form of the imaginary animals they create.*

OPPOSITE: Alebrije *dragon tail by Corelio Castellanos.*

 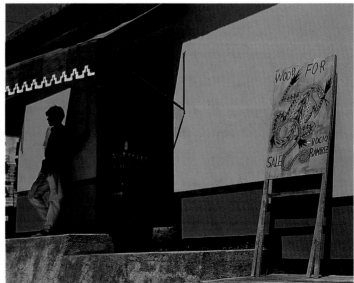

¡Tlayúda!

Take It Along!

There is too much of everything. Too many sounds and smells and colors. Too many people and too much food. The first-time visitor to the Mercado de Abastos gets caught in a current of sensations, pulled deep into a separate world, inescapable as a whirlpool.

Zapotec women balancing goods on their head bob easily beneath the low awnings that overhang the open stalls. Waves of market-goers coming from the opposite direction open up then close again around the more slow-moving tourists. The locals move purposefully and knowledgeably through aisle after aisle of stalls. For them this is not a casual outing, but life itself.

Sentimentality has no place at the market. A live turkey, destined for a holiday mole, is strapped upside down to a wooden cart. A sweet-faced woman, her hair in braids and wearing a dress of brilliant reds and blues, wields a machete, using short, sharp strokes to chop a stalk of fresh sugarcane. A butcher stands over a freshly killed pig that had spent that morning wallowing in the mud. Even the marigolds and cockscombs that will be used to decorate the altars of loved ones during the Day of the Dead are for the moment just another commodity, tossed onto the ground by sweating, swearing truck drivers.

Hundreds of voices hawking their wares—breads, sandals, chiles, and tortillas—join with the amplified sound of scores of boom boxes, each playing a different song. The sound is the din of commerce unleashed.

It takes a while to sort out the sensations, which is only understandable. After all, the Abastos

market, and the less frenetic weekly markets that take place in Tlacolula and Ocotlán, are part of an unbroken ritual that dates back thousands of years to Monte Albán. However, eventually a kind of clarity emerges from the tumult, even for the first-time market visitor. There is the almost dusty smell of unsweetened chocolate. In an aisle lined by chile vendors, huge burlap bags of dried ancho, chipotle, and chilhuacle negro (a dark, local variety) season the air with a smoky fragrance. The locals look quickly but carefully through the chiles, which are the critical ingredient in the sauces for which Oaxaca is justly famous.

With chocolate, little is left to chance. Some women still use a *metate*, a three-legged grinding stone, to bring the ingredients to the right consistency. Others return time and time again to a favorite *molino* (grinding mill) at the market, where the owner will pulverize and blend cacao beans, spices, and sugar into a perfect chocolate powder.

The market is a one-stop destination for just about anything Oaxaqueños need. The green-glazed pots used for mole are available. So are scrub brushes with Day-Glo-colored bristles, handwoven palm baskets, fine cutlery forged in town, and fresh pink-bodied *huachinango* (red snapper).

The items are on sale at multiple stands, making for fierce competition between vendors. It's hard to imagine that so many sellers of the same products can coexist. Picking up a couple loaves of bread, a bemused tourist asks its owner just how many bread vendors are at the market.

She looks back at him with a vaguely annoyed look, then scans the aisles of stacked bread around her. *"Hay bastante,"* she says. "There are enough."

Wheelbarrows full of fresh bread nearly overwhelm the visitor to Saturday's huge Abastos market, which is reputedly the largest in Central and South America.

ABOVE: *Available in colorful profusion—plastic shopping bags, water proof sandals, even kitchen brushes. Usually for sale outside the Palacio de Gobierno, the shopping bags are made by the families of Zapotec political prisoners from Loxicha, Oaxaca.*

OPPOSITE: *Wonderful pastels of lavender and lime-green decorate imposing stone columns that flank the mayor's office in Zaachila.*

Friends compare market finds in Tlacolula near the decorated gazebo in the town plaza. The national flag's colors are repeated in the papel picado *banners.*

Market day is seemingly every day in cities and villages across Oaxaca. Everything from groceries, apparel, handicrafts, and household items is for sale.

CLOCKWISE FROM TOP LEFT: Comparison shopping in Tlacolula.

A vendor travels north each month from the Isthmus of Tehuantepec, eager to sell her jewelry and richly embroidered traditional huipiles. Machine embroidery has unfortunately replaced much of the laborious handwork.

Chapulines (tiny fried grasshoppers) are a local delicacy sold in most markets. These salty, spicy, crunchy tidbits, teamed with the local brew, hit the spot at the end of the day.

No table is complete without the typical cheery Mexican oilcloth available in all markets.

A young carrizo (split bamboo) basket vendor pedals her store to market in Ocotlán.

Hammocks, both single and double, beckon with their brightly colored cotton or nylon threads.

RIGHT: *Handmade brooms and baskets at the market in Ocotlán.*

OPPOSITE: *This shopper's apron and* rebozo *headdress are common attire on market day. She balances her groceries in a locally produced basket, while carrying a new piece of pottery. However, imported plastic containers are making headway into the region and are replacing the handmade baskets and pottery.*

LEFT: *A grandmother teaches her granddaughter the fine points of shopping for sausages in the downtown 20 de Noviembre food market.*

OPPOSITE LEFT: *Chickens take on the shockingly bright golden color of the marigolds they are fed along with their corn diet.*

OPPOSITE RIGHT: *Clear-eyed fresh red snapper from the southern Oaxacan coast tempt passersby outside the Abastos market.*

Food markets

"To buy and sell, but above all, to commingle. In the old world, men make themselves two great excuses for coming together to a centre and commingling freely in a mixed, unsuspicious host. Market and religion. These alone bring men, unarmed, together since time began."

So writes D. H. Lawrence in "Market Day," one of the eight essays in his 1927 book *Mornings in Mexico*. In that statement he perfectly captures the ritual aspect of the Oaxaca markets and the central role that these gatherings play for the city.

In Oaxaca, the distinction between market and religion is sometimes obscured. Two of the city's markets, Benito Juárez and 20 de Noviembre, sit adjacent to San Juan de Diós. Built in the early 1520's, just after the conquest, it is considered the oldest church in Oaxaca. Its paintings reveal the valley at a spiritual transition, depicting the baptism of the last Zapotec ruler, Cocijoeza and the first mass performed in Oaxaca.

Vendors often stop at the church to pray for a successful day before beginning their long hours of selling. The sacred aspects of the markets are sometimes subsumed by the baser realities of commerce. The amber bodies of plucked chickens, their throats newly slashed, rest in piles at one stand. One vendor peddles dried grasshoppers and another haggles with a customer over the price of cow intestines dried to a jerky-like texture.

Yet the market's rituals are even older than those of the church. The smell of fresh tortillas rises from *comales*, cooking devices like griddles little changed since the days of Zapotec rule. The pottery, so beautiful and inexpensive that tourists just can't resist another purchase, originated not as art but as everyday utilitarian objects. And the faces of the vendors seem to be gazing not just over piles of marigolds, loaves of bread, and stacks of pomegranates, but across the centuries.

The Valley of Oaxaca produces vast quantities of large, beautiful fruits and vegetables. Interestingly, after the final performance at the Guelaguetza, participants toss various kinds of produce in a reenactment of gift-giving.

ABOVE: *Market food is hot, fresh, and delicious at the Abastos market. Oversized tortillas known as* tlayudas *are covered with toppings, or stuffed and cooked on a* comal.

OPPOSITE: *"¿Qué vá a llevar, Seño?" or "What can I offer you, miss?" is the common refrain at any market, interspersed with amplified announcements of specials, the blare of boom boxes, and the nervous wailing of roosters.*

PRECEDING PAGES: *Fresh herbs, spices, and livestock for cooking or for home remedies are shown here in a colorful array of pastels.*

ABOVE: *The Ocotlán Friday market is held just outside the former jail, which is now part of the Fundación Cultural Rodolfo Morales restoration complex.*

OPPOSITE: *Dried chiles are an integral part of most Oaxacan specialty sauces, and chile stands can feature a myriad of mysteriously labeled varieties, each known for its particular flavor or degree of hotness: chiles ancho, chilcostle, chilhuacle negro, chitepec, costeño, árbol, guajillo, mulatto, and pasilla, to name just a few!*

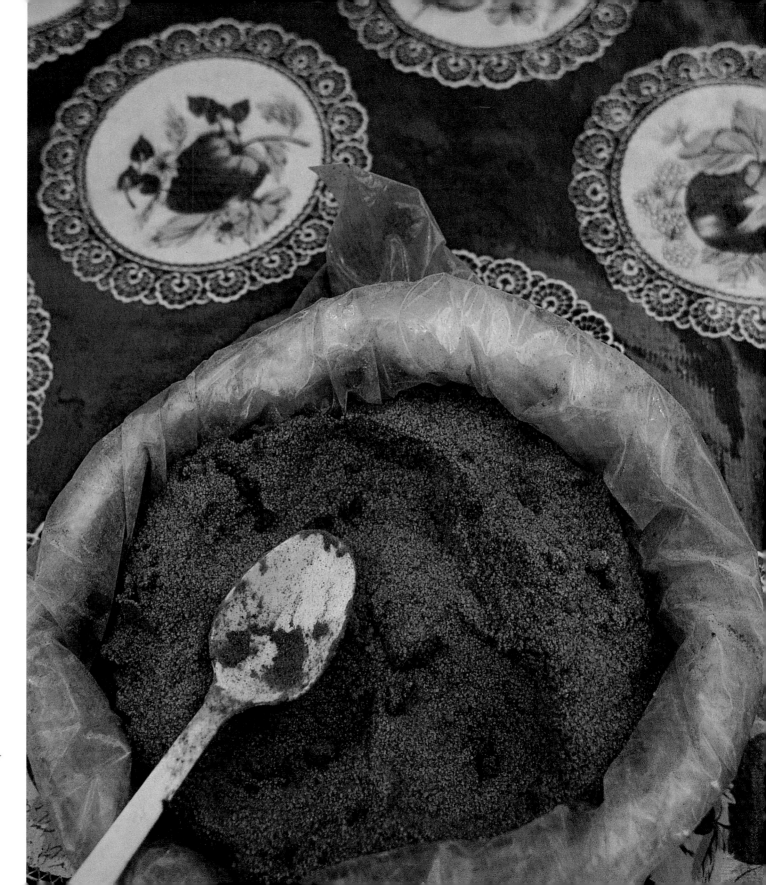

The dried chile is deseeded and deveined, ground into a powder, and sold by the kilogram. Or it can first be soaked in water until soft, then ground to a paste—in earlier times on a stone metate—these days in a blender, if available.

Roasted, then colored with vegetable dye, lowly pumpkin and squash seeds at the market in Ocotlán.

A delicious breakfast is created in the shape of a swallow (golondrina), with a tortilla beak, eggs for eyes, and avocados and papayas for the feathers and tail. Covered in a savory mild red chile sauce or refried beans, it is a visual and gustatory delight. Oaxacan cafés and restaurants offer specialties found nowhere else in Mexico, and the subtle combination of spices and herbs makes for memorable meals. Quesillo (string cheese), sopa de guias (a local vegetable soup), tasajo (thinly sliced grilled beef), moles, and tlayuda are all typical menu items.

RIGHT: *Paper flowers and tin mirrors encourage hungry customers to stop at an open-air* comedor *(restaurant), in the heart of the Abastos market.*

OPPOSITE: *A roving vendor in the Abastos market sells "everlasting" dried flower bouquets to take home.*

El Baile
del Espiritu

Dance of the Spirits

A lone calla lily rests atop a gravestone in the cemetery at Xoxocotlán outside of Oaxaca, its petals singed by the flame of a candle. The grave belongs to a small child who died many, many years ago. An old woman sits next to the tombstone. She wraps her arms tightly around her knees, and rocks slowly, her face hidden beneath a *rebozo* as she whispers to her baby, one of the *angelitos*, who according to tradition will return to earth this first night of Oaxaca's Day of the Dead celebration.

During the holiday, the solemnity of a funeral mixes with the lightness of a family reunion, even in a cemetery. Not far from the old woman, a man wearing a Los Angeles Lakers jacket hacks away at a cluster of agave plants that have overtaken his parents' plot. His children dust off the marker with their hands before they lean over and blow away the last bits of dirt. Then they begin placing marigold petals one by one on the inscribed stone until they create a cross. Their mother opens up an orange, and its spray of juice sparkles in the light of hundreds of candles that flicker in the graveyard. She bites into a piece, then places a couple of wedges on a gravestone. The orange's fresh smell joins briefly with the mingled sweet and spicy scent of flowers and copal, an incense burned since pre-Columbian times, drifting through the night air.

Oaxaca has become famous for one of Mexico's most beautiful Day of the Dead celebrations. Actually a three-day event, it coincides with Halloween and the Christian holidays of All Saints' Day and All Souls' Day and is the time of the year when the spirits of the dead are said to return to visit their loved ones. And so throughout the valley, rich and poor alike set up altars in their homes bedecked with sugarcane stalks and marigolds. They light candles on the altars and stock these tributes with

During the third week of July, the entire city celebrates traditional dance with performances in an event called La Guelaguetza. Villagers from the whole state don their best regional costumes to perform in the annual spectacle attended by thousands of thrilled viewers.

favorite foods and drinks of their dead relatives—sometimes even an open beer—to help guide the spirits back home.

The Day of the Dead is celebrated throughout Mexico, but other annual festivals, such as the Night of the Radishes on December 23, are unique to Oaxaca. The tradition supposedly began when vegetable vendors at a holiday market began to carve figures and scenes from the large radishes that grew in the area. The custom took hold and, in 1897, the city held the first official competition of carved radishes in the Zócalo.

Although the bawdier and more erotic carvings of past years are now rarely seen, the competition remains an entertaining event. Beneath the glittery holiday lights of the Zócalo, Oaxaqueños display multi-figure installations, from cancan dancers to scenes of the annual July folk dance festival, La Guelaguetza. During the dance event, villagers dressed in regional costumes perform local dances, from one celebrating the pineapple harvest in Alto Papaloapan Tuxtepec to a dance honoring the clay used in the pottery made in San Bartolo Coyotepec. Originating in a pre-Columbian ritual that honored the goddess of corn, Centeotl, the festival celebrates a longstanding cultural tradition of giving. The dance fiesta dates back to 1932, when it was held to honor the city's four-hundredth anniversary.

Oaxaqueños embrace all of the valley's distinctive festivals, but the Day of the Dead has a special importance. As the celebration progresses, even outsiders find themselves swept away by the complex emotions generated as life and death, laughter and tears, faith and superstition dissolve into pure belief. By the final day, when a breeze blows across the church plaza in Teotitlán del Valle just as the spirits are said to be departing the earth, skepticism is more dead than the dead themselves.

Early in March on Good Samaritan Day, many downtown businesses along the central corridor decorate booths with palm fronds and flowers, inviting everyone to receive aguas (sweet fruit drinks) in a reenactment of the biblical story of Jesus and the good Samaritan woman. Carrying their own cups, crowds form around decorated punch bowls as the local parish priest provides a blessing.

PRECEDING PAGES: *Traditional costumes dazzle at the* Lunes en el Cerro *(Monday on the Hill) Guelaguetza performance. This dancer's red yarn head covering (left) is a* rodete *(literally, "round pad"); the Yalalag crosses of her earrings are named after the town San Juan Yalalag. Their basic design, which predates the Spanish conquest, consists of a central cross from which hang three lesser crosses. After the final performance, the Guelaguetza stadium is awash with villagers from all over Oaxaca State. In fact, nearly half of Oaxacans are indigenous and speak one of Oaxaca's sixteen native languages.*

OPPOSITE AND ABOVE: *A beautiful Oaxacan girl is surrounded by her mother and aunts after their performance at the Guelaguetza (opposite). They are wearing the traditional* huipil *from Usila, a village of the Chinantec linguistic group in northeast Oaxaca. The term* guelaguetza *means "gift of appreciation" and dates from 1932, when Oaxaca celebrated its founding four hundred years earlier. At the end of each dance, performers toss gifts to the audience.*

Dancers concentrate on perfect precision and synchronicity. When the dancing is over, everyone joins in a Guelaguetza grand finale.

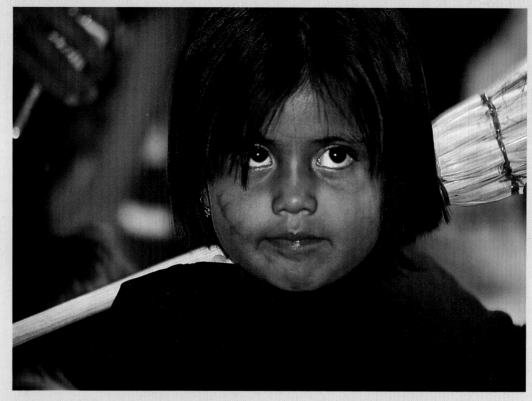

Day of the Dead

Despite coinciding with Halloween and the Christian holidays of All Saints' Day and All Souls' Day, the prominence of skeleton and skull imagery and the premise of the dead coming back to the earth strongly hint at the Day of the Dead's pre-Columbian roots.

Death has played a central role in Mexican religion for thousands of years. Individuals did not lose their earthly identities following death, nor were the dead presumed to exist in a realm completely separate from the living. Life and death were inseparable and reflected a dualistic worldview as represented by two gods: Quetzalcoatl, the god of life and the earth, and Michtlantecuhtli, the god of the dead and the underworld.

Two dates were set aside annually to honor the dead, and there is archaeological evidence of offerings in cemeteries that parallel the modern tradition of leaving food and drinks at gravesides and altars. Artwork, including a skull mask found at Monte Albán's Tomb 7 and a clay vase decorated with a skeleton, also illustrate the ceremonial role of death in native religions.

As part of their attempt to convert Mexico's indigenous peoples following the conquest, the Spaniards sought to absorb native beliefs into a Christian structure. But instead of the indigenous celebrations becoming Christianized, if anything, the Christian celebrations have been overtaken by Mexico's own ancient spirituality.

OPPOSITE: *A small child grows weary in his cleric's costume during a kindergarten Halloween parade around the Zócalo. North America's traditional Halloween celebration on October 31 has carved inroads into the time-honored Oaxacan Day of the Dead rituals, and many cartoon character costumes are for sale in the market.*

ABOVE: *An exhausted witch pauses during the kindergarten parade. From an early age, children take part in public performances that tend to culminate in the beloved Zócalo.*

ABOVE: *Small whimsical skulls made of sugar are personalized and exchanged between friends during the Day of the Dead festivities. Thousands of small clay figures are also available in a profusion of professions and activities. Incorporating devil imagery into these figures is a relatively modern concept.*

OPPOSITE: *Altars are personalized so that the appropriate spirit or soul will find its way back to its correct home during these special days. Here, a tiny nun is depicted, but a basketball player or a businesswoman with a cell phone could just as easily have been crafted. As the times change, so does the imagery.*

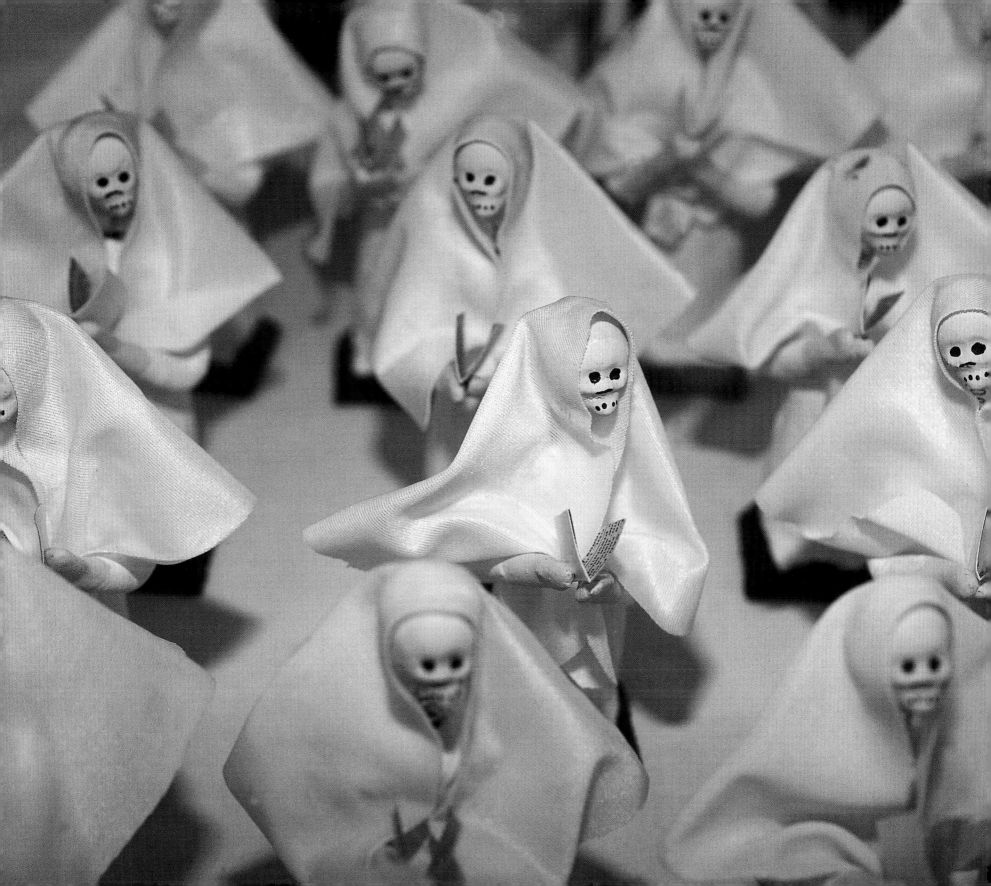

Calacas

In the weeks leading up to the Day of the Dead, Oaxaca is alive with skulls and skeletons (*calacas*). One would expect that the presence of so many bones, even ones made of plaster or ceramics, would create a decidedly morbid atmosphere.

But Oaxaca's skeletal spectacle is actually a joyous, comical rebuff to death. Children walk through town lapping at skulls made from sugar. The markets fill with figurines of painted tableaux made of clay showing skeletons engaged in a full range of human behavior: playing in mariachi bands and soccer games, driving sports cars, and sitting in a recliner drinking a beer and watching television. The figures play no formal or traditional role, but they certainly add to the levity of the celebration.

While images of skeletons and skulls date back to pre-Columbian times, these modern depictions were inspired by artist José Guadalupe Posada (1852–1913). Posada never formally studied art, but he worked as a lithographer and engraver at a newspaper before opening an illustration studio in Mexico City.

In his political and social commentaries, Posada often lampooned prominent individuals by depicting them as skeletons. Many of his prints were produced as broadsides and received wide circulation throughout Mexico. His works illustrated *corridos* or popular ballads that he collaborated on with publisher Antonio Venegas Arroyo and Oaxacan poet Constancio S. Suarez. The *corridos* featured illustrations and satirical song lyrics to portray current events and were performed by musicians who distributed the broadsides. Posada directed many of his most pointed works at the Oaxacan-born Mexican dictator Porfirio Díaz. Later Mexican artists including Diego Rivera and José Clemente Orozco cite Posada as a major influence.

ABOVE: *A solemn young boy sells a cheerful Day of the Dead hand puppet in the special "Muertos" market, which takes place the week or so before October 31 in the Abastos market.*

OPPOSITE: *Close-up of the papier-mâché sculpture "Catrina" by Miguel Linares.*

OPPOSITE: *Traditional Day of the Dead bread requires the addition of anise seeds and these special handmade, baked-in ladies made of flour. The bread is accompanied by warm bowls of hot chocolate redolent with cinnamon, ground almonds, and fresh cacao beans.*

ABOVE LEFT AND RIGHT: *Literally tons of marigolds (cempasuchil) and cockscombs arrive in the market to be sold for altar decoration. No one goes home without the necessary flowers for their private shrines dedicated to deceased loved ones and personal saints.*

Both public and private altars receive decorations of food, candles, Baby Jesus statues, and images of the Virgins of Soledad and Guadalupe. Organizations encourage altar building, as does the city, in an extravagant annual competition. The many night vigils in outlying neighborhoods and towns also honor the spirits with an array of sand paintings and decorated graves.

Mole

As the clock pushed toward eleven, someone at a gathering of Mexicans and visiting Americans finally asked what was for dinner. When he learned that a mole was on the menu, he and the other Mexicans just shook their heads.

"So late for mole," he said. "Her mole is delicious. But in a few hours when you are sleeping, it will explode in your stomach. Then do strange things to your dreams."

Until that odd and ominous statement, the Americans had regarded mole as simply a delicious sauce, albeit one closely linked with Oaxaca and the Day of the Dead. There are seven main varieties of mole (some a combination of twenty or more ingredients) and as many variations as there are cooks. Moles range from the smoky chocolate-brown of *mole negro* to the sweet flavor of golden *mole amarillo*. The sauce is most commonly served over fowl—although the mole itself is always the star.

While mole was likely prepared in pre-Columbian times, modern versions incorporate both native ingredients and items brought to Mexico by the Spaniards. Indigenous chiles are the prime element (*mole negro* is often made with five different kinds) but freshly made chocolate, along with nuts, pumpkin and sesame seeds, and fruits all contribute to the flavor. A pot of cooking mole is both richly fragrant and positively beautiful: a nearly perfect blend of these carefully ground ingredients prepared to the texture of liquid silk.

The whole process, from the selection of ingredients at the market to the hours simmering over a fire, can stretch for days: Mole is as much a ritual as it is a meal. So it was perhaps understandable that the mole served at the gathering arrived just a bit late.

And that night the Mexican gentleman's mole prophecy came true. The next morning the Americans compared dreams of strange flying creatures, like fanciful *alebrijes* (wood carvings), coming to life. Sensations of moving through other dimensions or across time. They would never again think of mole as just another sauce. Or eat it after midnight.

Above: *Margarita Mendoza Bautista roasts chiles on a comal for her Day of the Dead mole before daughter-in-law Aura prepares the complicated sauce that simmers for hours.*

Opposite: *Aura Bautista Lazo places her freshly prepared individual mole offering on the family altar in Teotitlán del Valle.*

An elderly woman takes one flower to her husband's graveside at Teotitlán del Valle.

FAR LEFT: *After the spirits finally depart at around three in the afternoon (at the chiming of the bells), the villagers in Teotitlán del Valle leave their homes and flock on foot and in cars to the cemetery to repair and decorate loved ones' graves and generally make merry; much food and drink is shared among neighbors, friends, even lucky strangers!*

LEFT: *Family members flew in from Tijuana to help with the cleanup and festivities at this fresh graveside.*

PRECEDING PAGES: Graves of loved ones are lovingly tended and decorated with handmade signs and flowers on November 2.

RIGHT: Conversations with the departed, at times fueled by the flowing mezcal, are a usual sight. Small groups of musicians also entertain through the night.

The inevitable specter of death is depicted on the south wall of Oaxaca's church of Santo Domingo.

ABOVE: *Individual candles light the graves of each niche and cast a warm golden glow along the wall of the city's public cemetery.*

OPPOSITE: *One young participant in the all-night vigil at Xoxocotlán is awash in candlelight and shares memories of the departed with family members. Many stay the entire night, including young children, keeping candles lit and spirits high.*

ABOVE LEFT AND MIDDLE: *Radishes take on a whole new meaning at the annual Noche de los Rábanos festival. Young and old try their hands in the radish-carving competition held on the Zócalo on December 23. Eventually, hundreds of carvings will be on public display.*

ABOVE RIGHT: *Christmas means calendas in the city of Oaxaca, and processions of these giant figures, the Monos de Calenda, parade through town on Christmas Eve before midnight mass. Originally, in 1741, Bishop Tomas Montano assembled a parade of these enormous figures representing the different races of the world to teach biblical precepts by allegory to the linguistically diverse population.*

OPPOSITE: *The posada is enacted the week before Christmas on the city's main streets: Sparklers and candles light the way for Joseph, Mary, and the shepherds.*

Schoolgirls giggle with delight and become girlishly shy.

This, of course, was a huge team effort. Many people, like threads, have woven in and out of the project. My initial inspiration and guidance came from Toni Sobel, an expatriot tour guide living in Oaxaca. It was she who observed that many of Oaxaca's finest artisans were already in their nineties and their work and stories needed to be recorded.

For holding my camera bag, taking notes or manning a reflector, I am indebted to travel companions past and present: Bill Steinmetz, Diana Judson, Gary Swenson, and Becky Robar. For professional encouragement, I am grateful to Lisl Dennis, travel photographer, and to Alejandro Tomás, photography instructor and personal friend. I have special gratitude for Jane Slater, Cynthia Wilder, and Kate Leiva for being the most supportive of friends. My agent, Judith Joseph, is an unfailing professional. An especially big thank-you to Bruce Whipperman for his vast pool of knowledge and great love of Oaxaca. Leslie Grace graciously provided missing specific cultural details. And to Matt "Mateo" Jaffe, *mil gracias* for your wonderful words and for being in that immigration line in Mexico City!

Working with Artisan has been a real pleasure. I am incredibly lucky to have a team there that includes Ann Bramson, publisher; Deborah Weiss Geline, editor; Nancy Murray, production; Burgin Streetman, publicity; and especially, Dania Davey, designer—a very special thank-you for the synergy created there. My sons, Christian and Andrew Haden, and my father, Robert Lawton Cooper, are a continual source of encouragement and sustenance. Thank you, Greg Peterson, for being such a loving, supportive second pair of eyes and ears both at home and in Oaxaca.

My interviews with Maestros Rodolfo Morales and Francisco Toledo gave me a considerably richer understanding of the complex issues of preserving culture and folk art and left me in awe of their civic participation and personal generosity. I had the opportunity to interview Rololfo Morales twice before his death in 2001; he is quite simply irreplaceable. I am extremely appreciative of the essential help provided by the Mexican Tourism Department as well as by José Calzadías and Armando Gamoneda of the Oaxacan State Tourism Office, and also to Luís Morán and AeroMexico. My *Lente de Plata* photographic award from former Mexican president Ernesto Zedillo sits proudly in my office in Seattle.

Finally, I am most grateful to the many Oaxacans who allowed me into their lives and homes. Their expansive spirits and generous welcomes made my task possible. Market vendors, artisans, shopkeepers, children, even night-vigil participants—there is much to be learned from the unspoken Oaxacan values of courtesy, patience, respect, and graciousness.